NORWICH
IN
50
BUILDINGS

PETE GOODRUM

AMBERLEY

For my very dear friend, the artist and Norwich man Keith Fox.

First published 2018

Amberley Publishing, The Hill, Stroud
Gloucestershire GL5 4EP

www.amberley-books.com

British Library Cataloguing in Publication Data.
A catalogue record for this book is available from the British Library.

ISBN 978 1 4456 6402 6 (print)
ISBN 978 1 4456 6403 3 (ebook)

Origination by Amberley Publishing.
Printed in Great Britain.

Contents

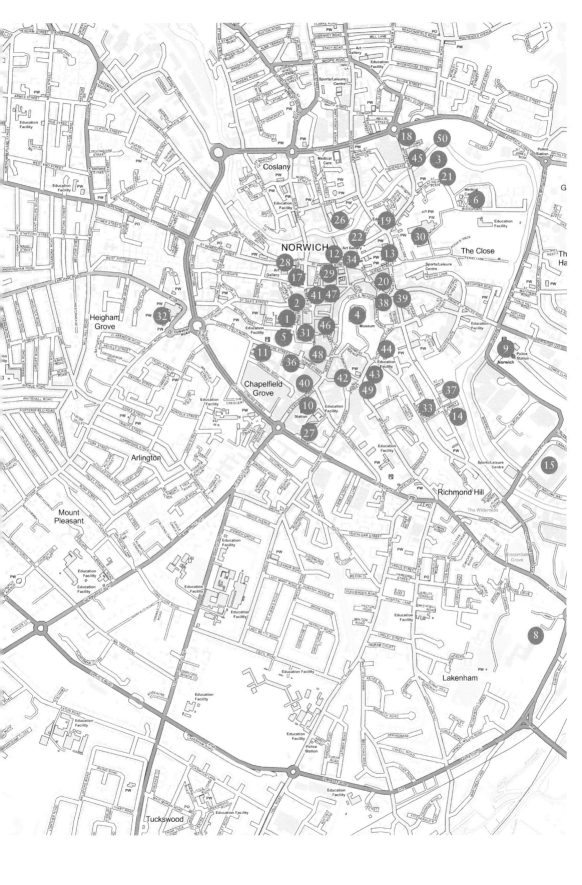

Key

Introduction

In writing this book I had more than one objective, but certainly high on the list was to *describe* fifty buildings in Norwich – their architecture was important. More than that, though, I wanted to write about how these buildings fit into the city and its history, to help paint a picture of the city and how it has evolved.

As I became immersed in the task I discovered something else: how so many of the buildings are connected with the story of Norwich itself. Their individual stories overlap in ways that even I – as a Norwich native – had not realised. I've not cross referenced these connections because, firstly, I didn't want to produce a book laden with footnotes and, secondly, because I hope that you'll enjoy discovering these coincidences and facts for yourself.

I have to make it clear that the buildings are of course a personal selection. With so many to choose from it was quite a challenge to get the list down to just fifty. Doubtless you will think of some you may have included and I've not. Hopefully I've included some that will come as a pleasant and informative surprise to you.

I began by trying to place the buildings within the book in some form of geographic order, grouping them into areas of the city. It proved difficult and rather ungainly, however. Alphabetical order was tempting, but not ideal. Eventually I decided to put them under headings that described their function or purpose. With some slight complications aside – such as the castle being both a museum and a place of civic history – I think it's worked and that it's made the book more navigable.

Historically, the castle and the cathedral, among others, are a great starting point. They are ancient places and underline the long history of the city. It's a story that continues with the rich wool merchants of the medieval period and continues into the grandeur of the eighteenth and nineteenth centuries. With the twentieth century come the City Hall, the Forum and the university. And now we're in the twenty-first century, where new projects and buildings will define the future.

Of the fifty buildings that I've chosen some have longer or more complex histories to be told than others, but they are all part of the unfolding story of Norwich. This book is in part a comment on the architecture of some of Norwich's buildings. But, more than that, I hope you will find it to be the story of Norwich *through* its buildings.

Pete Goodrum

The 50 Buildings

Civic and Government

1. City Hall

The origins of Norwich City Hall are quite clearly defined. Norwich Corporation, as it was at the time, had asked Robert Atkinson to prepare an outline, or layout, for a civic centre. Atkinson was a Cumberland-born man who had studied at the University of Nottingham before moving on to develop his skills in Paris, Italy and the USA. He would become known for his cinema building designs, with one of his most notable being the Regent Cinema in Brighton. This 3,000-seat picture house was built in the early 1920s and was claimed to be 'the first luxury cinema on the American model'. Ahead of its time, it included facilities to have tea and to dance. Perhaps his best-known work is the interior of London's *Daily Express*

City Hall.

building, which is renowned for its art deco style – a style that would find its way to Norwich and the City Hall.

Atkinson was appointed as judge for a competition that was launched in 1931 to find a design for the City Hall. Some 143 entrants were received and the commission was granted to Charles Holloway James and Stephen Rowland Pierce. James specialised in housing projects, but his partnership with Pierce, who had experience in town planning, was successful in creating civic buildings. Norwich City Hall is seen as perhaps their most important collaboration. Their designs were so noteworthy that they were exhibited at the Royal Academy in 1933. The Swedish influence on the concept is now seen as an indication of the 'between the wars' period. It was a fashionable approach and clearly references the tower of Stockholm City Hall.

Despite enthusiasm for the designs, the project became delayed because of complications in the planning process. The Depression of the early 1930s also served to slow things down. But, in 1936 the foundation stone was laid and work commenced in earnest. Two years later, on 29 October 1938, the building was officially opened by George VI and Queen Elizabeth, the Queen Mother.

A year later – 1939 – and the country was at war. Norwich would sustain terrible damage from bombing, although the City Hall remained intact. There has been speculation that its escape was no accident: Hitler had admired the building and perhaps even saw it as suitable for Nazi offices after an invasion. However, the facts are that, with 1945 and peace, the City Hall became the centre of Norwich's governance, which it had been intended for.

Embracing the police station, rates office, lord mayor's parlour and Council Chamber, it's never been anything other than impressive. The giant lions, designed by Alfred Hardiman, stand at the top of wide steps that lead to imposing bronze doors, featuring roundels depicting the history of Norwich. The clock tower stands as a real landmark on the Norwich skyline.

Norwich City Hall, is a Grade II-listed building and one of the 'Norwich 12' – a group of twelve Norwich buildings cited as being of particular historical and cultural importance. Perhaps its finest accolade is that the legendary architectural commentator Pevsner said it was 'the foremost English public building of between the wars … its siting and self confidence are its architectural triumph'.

2. Norwich Guildhall

Immediately opposite to it the Guildhall was, in effect, the predecessor to the City Hall. It was the seat of local government from its construction between 1407 and 1413 up to 1938, when the City Hall was opened.

The largest surviving medieval civic building outside London, the Guildhall is an essential part of Norwich history. It presided over the city during the

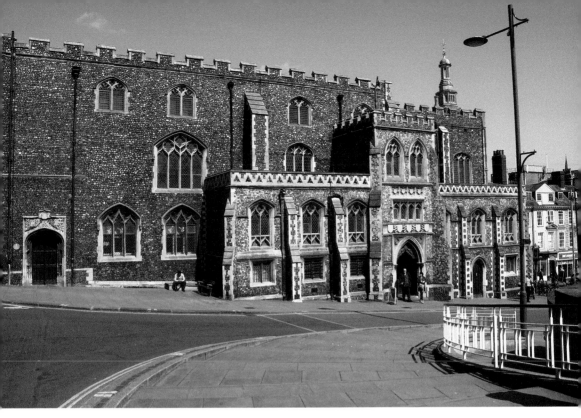

Norwich Guildhall.

period – in the 100 years or so from around 1650 – when Norwich was second only to London as a prosperous centre of trade.

The catalyst for the Guildhall's construction was the charter of 1404, which bestowed on the city considerable new powers of self-government, including having its own mayor. William Appleyard, freeman of the city, was the first to take the role; he was appointed just before the Guildhalll was built.

It's an interesting insight into life in the fifteenth century to note that until 1453 the windows were not glazed.

Strictly speaking, despite its great age, the Guildhall we see today is not entirely as it was built. In 1511, the roof of the original Council Chamber collapsed, and it brought down with it two towers built of timber and tile that stood on the north and south ends of the building. Repairs were commissioned and by 1534 a new Council Chamber was in place. At the same time the outside walls were faced with the characteristic chequered flint so redolent of Norwich and Norfolk, and adorned with the arms of Henry VIII, accompanied by the arms of Norwich and the St George's Company.

Further modifications were carried out in the nineteenth century when the city surveyor, Thomas Barry, made some additions to the south side of the building. Later still, in 2010 restoration work was done to strengthen the clock tower.

Throughout all of this, and until the City Hall was opened, the Guildhall provided the city with a courtroom, gaol, chapel, administrative offices,

The Guildhall's chequered flint, so redolent of Norwich and Norfolk.

a strongroom and even storage for the city's civic regalia. In the nineteenth century a police station was incorporated into the building. The Guildhall had long been a place where prisoners were kept. In fact, the undercroft, where some were held, is thought to be even older than the Guildhall itself. As early as 1531, the Protestant priest Thomas Bilney had been detained there prior to his being burned at the stake at Norwich's notorious Lollard's Pit. This important building has a less sinister role today. The café on the ground floor is a popular meeting place.

Understandably, the Guildhall is another member of the 'Norwich 12'.

3. Norwich Crown and County Courts

The Guildhall has long since ceased to be the seat of law in the city. Nowadays the Norwich Crown and County Courts are housed in custom-designed premises in Bishopgate. The purpose-built and multi-function courts were not constructed until the early 1980s, but preparing the ground for them in 1981 led to a remarkable insight into Norman Norwich. An archeological dig revealed the remains of a cellar that had been part of a significant twelfth-century house. An indication of the sophistication of the ancient residents is the so-called 'latrine

Norwich Crown and County Courts.

Magistrates' Court.

tower'. An arch at the base of the tower was open to the river. As it was still tidal there, the river would have effectively 'flushed' the toilet twice every day.

The remains of the Norman house are so important that they have been preserved in a special basement beneath the Magistrates' Court part of the complex.

4. Norwich Castle

The castle could, of course, have appeared in the 'Museums' section of this book because it's been a world-class museum for decades; however, it's performed more duties for the city over the centuries before that.

The castle was established by William the Conqueror after his 1066 invasion. By 1075 it must have been completed as it's in that year that it's mentioned in accounts of an uprising against William. Over the centuries the castle would be at the centre of other skirmishes, including the revolt against Henry II in 1173. It would see the end of Kett's Rebellion when, on 7 December 1549, Robert Kett was hanged from the castle's walls. By the nineteenth century, when those walls were being repaired and restored in a Victorian transformation, opinions on Kett had also been transformed. More enlightened viewpoints now positioned him as not so much guilty of treachery, but more a hero of the people.

The reality is that rebuilding, demolition, refacing and conversions have rendered the castle as something quite different from its original manifestation.

Norwich Castle.

And yet, much of the work has been sympathetic; for example, the 1830s work on the keep retains (or is at least based on) the original decoration.

When centuries of use as a gaol and place of execution ended, the museum took over and rapidly established itself as somewhere of national and international importance. It houses collections of art, ceramics and textiles, as well as exhibits dating from the Vikings and the time of Boudica – that earlier leader of a Norfolk rebellion.

It had opened as a museum in 1895, with the conversion from a gaol having been started in 1887. The city council had bought the castle and the work was carried out by Edward Boardman.

Now a Grade I-listed building, Norwich Castle is also a Scheduled Ancient Monument. An integral part of the city's landscape for approaching a thousand years, it's as vibrant now as a place of discovery as it once was imposing as a centre of control over Norwich and its citizens.

5. The Forum

On the other side of City Hall, and standing with as much contrast to the ancient Guildhall as it's possible to imagine, is The Forum. This large and impressive building became part of the city centre's architecture as the result of a tragedy.

Since the early 1960s the site had been occupied by the library, which had replaced the old Free Library at the corner of St Andrews and Duke Street. The new

The Forum.

building was very much of its time and was home to the city library as well as the 2nd Air Division Memorial Library. Funds for this had been raised as early as 1945 by crews and personnel of the American 2nd Air Division, who had been stationed here during the war. It was a mark of gratitude for the way in which the city had welcomed the Americans during the 'friendly invasion' of the war.

When the new library was opened in 1963 the 2nd Air Division Memorial Library was incorporated into it and opened to the public. It contained a roll of honour and literature on aspects of American life. A memorial fountain in keeping with the modern architecture was also built in the courtyard and the building contained stones from every one of the American states.

It seemed that a new building had been constructed to become a long-standing part of the city's heart. It wasn't to be, however. With a terrible irony, given its links to wartime Norwich, it was destroyed by fire. On 1 August 1994 fire crews rushed to what would become one of the biggest conflagrations in the city's long and tumultuous history. Over 150,000 books were destroyed, along with other precious documents. It seemed that, in this most literary of cities, the library was lost. But, out of the ashes rose the Forum.

In fact, the need to build brought an added blessing. Before construction began there was the opportunity to carry out archeological investigations. A twentieth-century building had been destroyed and now it was possible to look back before looking forward.

After the Norman invasion the area had been settled by French merchants, becoming known as 'the French Borough'. Now there was a chance to learn more about Norwich in the 1070s. In the meantime, aided by Lottery funds and as a Millennium Project for the east of England, award-wining architect Sir Michael Hopkins set about designing the new building. His was a brave vision of a courtyard within a giant horseshoe-shaped three-storey building. There would be bow string steel trusses creating leaf-shaped panels to support the courtyard roof, natural light would flood in to a spectacular atrium, load-bearing brickwork would carry giant balconies, and it would house the various departments and functions of the multipurpose building, which would, of course, contain the library.

The concept became a reality, and the Forum was opened to the public in 2001, with Her Majesty the Queen officially opening it in 2002. A truly twenty-first century building of great imagination had been erected in the very heart of the city, standing in happy contrast with its ancient neighbours.

6. The Great Hospital

The Great Hospital is an important building for a variety of reasons: it has one of the smallest monastic cloisters in England, it's a site of architectural and historic interest, and it's deeply enshrined in the history of Norwich.

The Great Hospital.

Bishop Walter de Suffield founded the Great Hospital in 1249. The concept was rooted in the Augustinian model, which sought to contain the amount of liturgy and ritual carried out so that more time could be given to charitable work.

The charitable work, or objectives, of the Great Hospital were clearly defined as taking care of 'aged priests, poor scholars and sick and hungry paupers'. Some thirty beds were provided for the sick, and paupers – thirteen of them – were to be fed at the gates every day. In a commendable spirit of meritocracy, poor boys were fed and given a chance of education with the hope that they might become choristers or priests. The care of aged priests was an important issue because as they were not allowed to marry they usually had no family to care for them in old age.

In 1383, Richard II and his wife, Anne of Bohemia, came to Norwich. The hospital contains over 250 ceiling panels featuring black eagles, which are thought to have been painted to mark the visit. The panels were moved in the sixteenth century when the building was altered – the church was divided into two wards.

Today the Great Hospital is of considerable interest to scholars and academics, being one of the oldest hospitals in the country. It still functions as a retirement home, but its buildings and archives form a rare insight into medieval England.

At that time The Great Hospital was one of a thousand or more such institutions in the country. There was little or no specific medical treatment as we know it. A holistic approach to wellbeing was at the core of its philosophy, with care of the soul being a main aim. Indeed, the very creation of such a hospital was seen as a benefit to the spiritual health of its founder. Caring and tending to the needs of patients as it did, the hospital bore little resemblance to its modern descendant.

7. Norfolk and Norwich University Hospital

In 1771, with the founding of the Norfolk and Norwich Hospital, Norwich moved into a new era. Modernised and extended throughout the nineteenth century, the 'N and N' in its red-brick building on St Stephens Road became a part of Norwich life. It continued to be so as it grew throughout the 1960s and 1970s.

In October 2002 a service was held in Norwich Cathedral as a thanksgiving for the hospital and its contribution to the city and county. Work and relocation had already started but by 2003 the last departments had shipped out to the new Norfolk and Norwich University Hospital at the Norwich Research Park.

Tony Blair, then prime minister, had announced the go ahead for the new hospital in a live TV broadcast from Tokyo as part of the *Breakfast with Frost* show on 11 January 1998. It would be the first new NHS teaching hospital in the UK for thirty years. Work on the site began the next day.

A second phase to increase the size of the hospital was unveiled as early as 2000. In 2001, over budget but ahead of schedule, the hospital was completed.

Norfolk and Norwich University Hospital.

The award-winning project – it won the Building Better Healthcare Prize for Best Designed Hospital in 2002 – was overseen by architects Anshen & Allen, with John Laing plc as the main contractor.

To describe the NNUH as 'a building' is a massive understatement. In the spirit of this book it is a 'building' of enormous significance to Norwich, but in reality it is a vast site and group of buildings including wards, an accident and emergency department, specialist departments, a Day Procedure Unit, outpatients facilities and research departments.

With affiliations to the Medical School and the University of East Anglia, the hospital is a thriving place, with over 7,000 staff caring for more than 800,000 Norfolk people every year.

5. County Hall

The original Norfolk and Norwich Hospital was the place of work for Dr Philip Martineau. An eminent surgeon, he practised there for more than fifty years. He was born in 1752, and by the time he died in 1829 he had acquired substantial assets. County Hall stands on land that was part of his estate and Martineau Lane is named after him.

Above: County Hall.

Below: County Hall. (Courtesy of R. G. Carter Group Archive)

The eleven-storey building on Martineau Lane, home to Norfolk County Council, is seen as an important example of the international style for municipal architecture. Highly visible in the surrounding landscape on the edge of the city, it was designed by Reginald Uren. Uren had already established a reputation, having worked on the award-winning Hornsey Town Hall in 1935. These were the times of Swedish influence, which is noticeable in James and Pierce's work for Norwich City Hall. Other relevant architectural influences on County Hall would be the Sanderson building in London in which, like County Hall, Uren made positive moves towards a post-war style. County Hall stands out for its different use of the 'curtain wall' feature, which is seen as a defining point in this style of architecture. It also does not use the then fashionable sheet materials such as aluminium and steel, but instead features brick and glazed ceramic cladding. It is, in fact, despite it giving such a first impression, not at all typical of a 1960s building. And yet it is one. Designed in 1966, it was built over two years at a cost of £2.5 million and opened by Her Majesty Queen Elizabeth II on 24 May 1968. She was greeted by Bob Carter of R. G. Carter, who had carried out the building work.

Transport

9. Norwich (Thorpe) Railway Station

The 1830s and 1840s had seen huge investment in the railways. All over the country, small independent companies built lines and then often merged into larger operations. Norfolk was no exception. By April 1844 the Yarmouth &

Norwich (Thorpe) railway station.

Above: The station's great dome – 76 feet high and covered in zinc tiles.

Below: This rare and previously unpublished photograph shows the booking hall at Norwich station, which was built by John Youngs, now part of the R. G. Carter Group. It is seen here soon after its completion in 1886. (Courtesy of R. G. Carter Group Archive)

Norwich Railway, with £200,000 worth of share capital issued by an Act of Parliament, was up and running. The efficiency of its construction programme may well have been the result of its chairman being the legendary railway pioneer George Stephenson and its chief engineer being his equally famous son Robert.

The Yarmouth & Norwich Railway had built the original station on the site at Thorpe, but regular passenger services and ever-increasing traffic meant that something bigger was needed. Designs were prepared by William Neville Ashby. Only a few years earlier he had left his job with Edward Wilson & Co., who had done much work on the early railways, to join the Great Eastern Railway, who now operated the Norfolk services. His colleague John Wilson followed him and together they started work on the free Renaissance styling for Norwich's new terminus.

It was a building that was both decorative and functional. It drew on local contractors, such as Barnard, Bishop & Barnard to provide decorative ironwork, and Dixons & Co. of London Street, Norwich, who supplied the clock that was to be installed in the imposing clock tower. The building work itself was carried out by Youngs & Son – now part of the R. G. Carter Group.

The new building was opened in 1886. With its platform canopies and track design that did away with earlier shunting methods, this was the face of the modern railway.

1c. The Bus Station

There has been a bus station in Norwich's Surrey Street for decades. The original one was built by the Eastern Counties Omnibus Co. in 1936 to replace outdated garages at their Cremorne Lane depot. With space for 180 vehicles, a waiting room, lost property office and cafeteria it was everything a 1930s bus station should be. It also had a claim to fame: it had the largest roof unsupported by pillars in Europe. A precedent for this had been set, it seems, because when the pre-war bus station was replaced its successor would also have a notable roof. The impressive steel roof of the new station was a key part of it winning the 2006 SCALA Civic Building of the Year Award. The new bus station opened in 2005 at a cost of £5 million, but it was not instantly welcomed by everyone and was not without controversy.

Norwich architect Michael Spicer's design would go on to be named by *Design Curial* magazine as 'one of the top ten bus stations in the world'. When that was announced the *Eastern Daily Press*, among others, expressed some surprise, calling the bus station 'controversial' and claiming that the accolade had been awarded 'despite problems with its leaky roof'. It wasn't an entirely unfounded jibe as the station had to be closed for a while in 2012 for the leaks to be fixed. More controversy would follow when the bus station suffered from being overcrowded. On the positive side, though, that overcrowding was an indication of its popularity.

The bus station.

With commendable environment-friendly design features, including low-energy lighting and natural ventilation, the bus station has fourteen bus stands configured around a central travel centre and handles some 200,000 passengers a week.

But it's the roof that marks it out as a building in Norwich. Protected by translucent material, the impressive structure is triangular with a hexagonal light well. Some say that the real drama of the design is not sufficiently apparent from the ground. However, controversy aside, it is a stunning building and very impressive bus station.

Entertainment

11. Theatre Royal

Being only a short walk from the Assembly House, its near neighbour, the Theatre Royal, is another example of how buildings in Norwich can exist in harmony despite being in radically different styles.

The modernity of the Theatre Royal building does rather belie it being a theatre that first opened in 1758. Just four years after Thomas Ivory had begun his renovation of the Assembly Rooms in 1754, Norwich was opening the doors of its new theatre just yards away. The builder, as well as sole proprietor, was Thomas Ivory.

Theatre Royal.

Raising £600 from Norwich businessmen, architect, timber merchant and master builder Thomas Ivory became the owner of the New Theatre.

The building was very close to where today's theatre stands and would become the home of the Norwich Company of Comedians, who had previously based themselves at the White Swan Inn.

Ivory died in 1799 and, as the new century began, the Theatre Royal was remodelled by the builder and architect William Wilkins. It was Wilkins's son who built the second Theatre Royal in 1826 at a cost of £6,000.

The nineteenth century would see the installation of gas lighting, which was to be replaced by new electric lighting in 1894. Despite various legal wrangles over licenses and constant changes to the entrance and exit facilities, the theatre flourished for decades until in June 1934 when it was destroyed by fire.

Just over a year later the new building – the one that stands today – was opened. The speed with which it was built was greatly helped by it being based on an existing design, already used for Odeon cinemas.

The building, unlike some nearby properties, escaped serious damage during the war and, with peace and the 1950s, developed into a cinema as well as a theatre. Its one-time rival the Hippodrome was demolished in 1966 some years after going out of business, but the Theatre Royal adapted and survived, bringing in a huge range of acts and productions. By 1967 Norwich City Council had purchased the Theatre Royal with plans to create a multipurpose civic theatre. More legal arguments ensued, but while the operational plans were halted the theatre was closed in 1970 to allow work on a major refurbishment.

December 1972 saw the Gala reopening and the beginning of another chapter. The next few years would see the old rehearsal room in a Victorian church turned into a theatre, the establishment of the Theatre Arts course by the then manager Dick Condon, and in 1991 the start of yet more improvements to the building. Norwich City Council architect Jim Meering oversaw the construction of new office space, alterations to front of house and a new blue and gold colour scheme for the auditorium.

The twenty-first century would see changes in both the building and the management of the Theatre Royal. In 2003, the management was merged with that of the Playhouse, and in the following year the Theatre Arts Courses had found a home in The Garage.

In 2006, the administration, marketing and box office departments had also found a new home: in Dencora House, immediately next door to the theatre. And soon, in early 2007, more work effectively joined the two buildings, simultaneously creating the opportunity to reconfigure the entire frontage. Now came the new bars, restaurant, toilets, lifts and glass balcony. With improved ventilation, concert hall standard acoustics and new seating, the Theatre Royal was in excellent shape to celebrate its 250th anniversary in 2008.

Maintaining a world-class theatre will always mean a constant programme of improvements and modernization, but the Theatre Royal has never flinched from the need to change and adapt. It is a vital part of the city's cultural heritage and future.

12. The Playhouse

The Theatre Royal and the Playhouse are closely linked, having been in an arrangement of joint management since 2003.

Since its opening in 1995, the Playhouse has established itself as an important venue with a national reputation. Creating the venue by converting the building was a six-year project. Local architects Lambert, Scott & Innes worked closely with the Playhouse founder Henry Burke and Theatre Projects. Some 80 per cent of the £2.5 million costs came from local businesses and individuals – their names are inscribed on bricks inside the building as a mark of gratitude.

The Playhouse opened to rave reviews – not just for performances, but for the building itself. Its acoustics and sightlines, the disabled access and its much vaunted open-ended stage all met with approval.

The Playhouse today is one of the most well-respected performance venues in the country. However, the history of this solid red-brick building in St George's Street threads through the story of Norwich.

It had certainly seen service as a maltings in the nineteenth century, and later became the Crown public house. England's first provincial newspaper, *The*

The Playhouse.

Norwich Mercury, had been established in the 1700s, and it also used this building as its premises in the nineteenth century.

The building would also serve as a restaurant and a storage facility for a motorcycle dealer, but before that it was also home to Ruymps. Founded in 1795, the builders' merchants, who for a while occupied the land that would become Norwich City FC's 'Nest', were an integral part of so many buildings and projects in Norwich.

13. The Samson and Hercules

The Samson and Hercules is a place that's woven into the social history of Norwich. It's named after the two statues that stand at the doors of the property. There had been an earlier building on the site, but around 1657 a new house was erected there by Christopher Jay, who was then mayor of Norwich. He incorporated some of the original structure and installed Samson and Hercules, the two great figures, to support the porch of his new house. They remained there for well over 100 years, until in 1789 they were taken away and stored at the rear of the building.

At some point over a century later the property had been acquired by local businessman and antique dealer George Cubitt. He decided to refurbish the

The Samson and Hercules.

building and planned to return the statues to their duties at the front of the building. Samson was fine, but Hercules wasn't. In too bad a condition to be restored, Hercules was replaced and has been a replica of the original since then.

For the first decades of the twentieth century the building was put to a myriad of uses, including Cubitt himself operating his furniture business there, an excise office, a medical practice, and a YMCA in the 1920s. In the 1930s it was a swimming pool in summer and a ballroom in winter.

The Samson and Hercules Ballroom rapidly established itself as the place to be. Cashing in on the massive popularity of ballroom dancing it rode out the war years, attracting American servicemen stationed around Norfolk.

Surviving a fire, the Samson (as it was known) was effectively rebuilt in the 1950s when it was still the city's premiere ballroom dancing venue. And it remained a favourite when the foxtrot and waltz gave way to the twist in the 1960s.

Eventually, and inevitably, it adjusted itself again to be part of the nightclub scene. Ritzy's opened its doors for a new generation to enter under the watchful eyes of the two old statues. Sadly, in the mid-1990s a terrible accident occurred: Samson's arm fell off.

The venue went on to become another club, the Ikon, but by the end of the twentieth century the namesake guardians were tired. Fibre glass replicas replaced Samson and Hercules, who went into retirement. The building would stand empty

The statues outside the entrance.

for a period, during which the replica statues were painted in bright colours for an art show.

Restoration work, a public campaign and Lottery funding have continued the story of the statues. The building has waxed and waned over the years, but despite its long history it is the twentieth century that it will be most remembered for – because of dancing.

14. The Waterfront

In truth, the Waterfront is not the most imposing of buildings. But it's not its architecture that earns it a place in this collection of fifty buildings in Norwich, it's the place it plays in the cultural history of the city and the status it enjoys.

In a way the Waterfront is a logical descendant of the Samson and Hercules. The Samson, along with the Gala and the (much renamed) Melody Rooms are among others places that have defined generations. It was in these halls and discotheques that the young people of Norwich danced and saw the musical stars of their day perform.

The ballroom dances of the 1940s, the jiving of the 1950s and the dance crazes of the 1960s were all long gone by 1990, when Norwich City Council set up the Waterfront as a venue. By 1993 it was not looking like a success and it was at that point that the running of the place was taken over by the Union of UEA Students. It was not to be run as a student club, however. In fact, a quarter of a century later, the Waterfront has a justifiable claim as Norwich's favourite live music venue. The list of acts that have appeared there is impressive to say the least and include the Arctic Monkeys, Amy Winehouse, Elbow, Nirvana, Courtney Pine, Paul Weller, Radiohead and Pulp.

In contrast to the 'big names', the Waterfront also presents new bands and works with local promoters and provides real support to the city's and county's music community.

Alternative and indie nights, the nationally renowned Rock 'n' Roll Party PROPAGANDA, and club nights on Saturdays are all part of the venue's now long-established credentials.

It's not about the building itself, it's about what happens there. It's an important part of Norwich.

The Waterfront.

15. Norwich City Football Club's Carrow Road Stadium

Norwich City FC are, of course, known as the Canaries. Their first ground was on Newmarket Road. They began playing there in 1902, but in 1908 – the year they recorded a record attendance of 10,366 – they fell into a quarrel with the owners over renting it. Unable to resolve the matter, the club moved to what had been a chalk quarry in Rosary Road. It soon earned the nickname of the Nest – what else for the Canaries?

The Nest had obvious limitations from the outset: there was never going to be room to expand the facility and disused chalk quarries are prone to problems. As early as the mid-1920s the club was looking at other options, and subsidence resulting in a corner of the pitch falling away made the need all the more urgent.

By 1935 the Nest was in a bad state of repair and the Football Association made it clear that they considered the ground unsafe and inappropriate. Their letter to the club did not pull any punches. It said that the Nest was 'no longer suitable for large crowds and measures must be taken'. With only weeks until the start of the new season the Canaries not only had to fly the Nest, but they had to find another home. They found the Boulton and Paul sports ground in Carrow Road (less than a mile away), a site owned by J. & J. Colman.

What happened next is, deservedly, part of Norwich legend. It's a story that moves with breathtaking speed. On 1 June 1935 Colmans sold the lease of the land to Norwich City FC. On the day of the sale tenders were put out for the work and on 11 June construction work was started. Rubble from demolishing the Nest

Norwich City FC's Carrow Road Stadium.

was used to build the bank that would form the 'River End' at Carrow Road. By
17 August most of the stands had been built. With building work still going on
around them, the club played a practice game on 26 August.

When West Ham came to Carrow Road on 31 August 1935 there were 29,779
people in the ground to watch the game. The club was open for business. It had
taken just eighty-two days to build a stadium.

From those first days of pre-war football Carrow Road has seen many changes.
In 1979, R. G. Carter completed the new River End and would go on to construct
the City Stand in 1988 and the Barclay in 1992. In 2004, they completed the
South Stand, replacing the original that they'd built in 1935.

In times of market diversification Carrow Road, like many stadiums, has
hosted concerts. It's pulled in big names, including Elton John, Status Quo and
Rod Stewart. But it's really about football. Pundits have their various views about
Norwich City's place in the world of football. But, in Norwich, the Canaries are a
vital part of the city's life. And Carrow Road is their home.

16. Eaton Park's Buildings

Norwich is blessed with parks and green spaces, and typical of them is Eaton
Park. While it was refurbished with Heritage Lottery funds in 1988, the park's
history began in the early twentieth century. The Corporation, or Norwich City
Council as it's now known, embarked on a programme of acquiring land with the
intention of developing recreational and sports parks. As part of that initiative, in

Below and opposite: Eaton Park's buildings.

1906 they bought the 80 acres of fields and market gardens that would become Eaton Park for £900 – some of the funds were made available by the Norwich Playing Fields and Open Spaces Society.

For various reasons, not least of which was the First World War, the land lay undeveloped for some years, although it was one of the venues to host the Royal Norfolk Show in its pre-Norfolk Showground days.

The peace that followed the First World War did not immediately bring prosperity. Unemployment soared, so to counteract it the Corporation, aided by government funding, created a form of unemployment relief by putting men to work in establishing the parks.

The design was based on proposals submitted in 1924 by Captain Sandys-Winsch, the superintendent of Norwich City Parks and Gardens.

More than 100 men worked for over three years to build the grand sweeping pavilions, bandstand and lake for model boats. They stand as a testament to that grand plan. They added the football pitches, tennis courts and bowling greens to make Eaton Park complete, and in May 1928 the grand opening was conducted by the Prince of Wales.

17. The Maddermarket Theatre

Tucked away in St Johns Alley, the Maddermarket is a Norwich institution. Its existence is almost entirely down to one man. Walter Nugent Bligh Monck had had a reasonably successful career in the London theatre when he came to Norwich in 1909 to direct some historical tableaux at St Andrew's Hall. He also took on the direction of masques at Blickling Hall and somehow gravitated to Norwich.

After service in the Royal Army Medical Corps during the First World War, he set about finding a home for the company of amateur actors he'd established as far back as 1911. In 1921, his search led to a building that had started life as a Catholic chapel and seen service as a baking powder factory. The acoustics of the building were what attracted Monck most. Naming it after the adjacent Church of St John the Baptist Maddermarket, Monck began producing plays on a stage that replicated the Renaissance theatre. The Maddermarket had created the first permanent stage of that type since the Restoration in the 1660s.

With his strict rules and firm views, Monck steered the company through the 1930s and '40s. While escaping damage in the air raids on Norwich, the building was proving too small to accommodate the growing audience numbers. In 1948, a plan was mooted to refurbish the warehousing and storage areas as well as, crucially, extending the building to enlarge the auditorium.

Fifteen years later, in 1964, the theatre underwent more dramatic modifications. A bigger wardrobe and rehearsal room were provided, new cloakrooms were added, together with the bar and foyer areas. Juxtaposed with the Elizabethan appearance of the original building, these extensions represent the face of the theatre as it's seen today.

Right and below: The Maddermarket
Theatre.

Always developing and with a repertoire today that is much broader than Mr Monck's original concept, the Maddermarket is a building that occupies an ancient site, has grown and developed with the changing city, and stands with some of the most important cultural output of Norwich.

18. The Puppet Theatre

Strictly speaking, as a building this belongs in the Religious Buildings section: St James is a medieval church after all. But it was here that Ray and Joan DaSilva chose as the permanent home for their touring company.

Founded in 1979, the Norwich Puppet Theatre actually opened its doors in December 1980. Today it's one of just three building-based puppet theatres in England. With a 175-seat auditorium as well as workshops, a shop and a bar, the Puppet Theatre is a venue for performances as well as somewhere to learn about making puppets. The combination of venue and purpose makes the Norwich Puppet Theatre unique and of international importance.

St James' Church is a magnificent example of a fifteenth- and sixteenth-century church. Its flint and stone construction, so redolent of Norwich and Norfolk, and its three-stage tower mark it out as a significant part of the city's religious and architectural heritage. The vibrancy of the Puppet Theatre's diverse and exciting work position it among the most important places of entertainment in the city.

The Puppet Theatre.

Hotels and Inns

19. The Maids Head Hotel

Opposite the Samson and Hercules, and predating it by four centuries, the Maids Head Hotel can trace its origins back to the thirteenth century. It's been a Grade II-listed building since 1954 and, the architecture aside, it's a place that features prominently in Norwich's history. The famous Paston letters were written there (at least in part); Catherine of Aragon, Henry VIII's first wife, stayed there; in 1549 during Kett's Rebellion troops from both sides claimed it; and it comes as no surprise to learn that Norfolk's famous Parson Woodforde dined and drank there, recording it in his diary in 1791.

The famous 'Tudor' frontage is definitely mock Tudor, however, as it didn't arrive until the 1890s. It was commissioned by Mr Walter Rye, who had been a customer and the lease holder until he acquired the property, seemingly driven by a desire to preserve its atmosphere as much as its architecture.

In the 1930s the hotel is mentioned in J. B. Priestly's *English Journey*, and it continues to crop up in literature and film across the decades.

Expanding and modernising since it took over adjoining premises in the 1950s, The Maids Head is now a twenty-first-century hotel with a spectacularly historic location. And, of course, among its oak panels there are still legends

The Maids Head.

Detail work on the building.

of hauntings: an elderly man, possibly a former lord mayor, shakes his head in the courtyard; and a whiff of lavender warns of a ghostly maid approaching from centuries past. None of them seem to have any effect on the popularity of The Maids Head.

2c. The Royal Hotel

This imposing building intriguingly links together several aspects of Norwich and its buildings. It was the hotel built to replace the old Royal, formerly The Angel, which had stood on the site now occupied by the Royal Arcade.

The need for such an impressive and well-appointed hotel at the top of Prince Of Wales Road was inextricably linked to the growth of the railways – the city's terminus is at the bottom end of the road.

Its construction necessitated the demolition of several older properties and yet this nineteenth-century modernisation led to the builders discovering parts of the city's ancient heritage in forgotten sections of the castle's outer reaches.

Work on the site and the building would have been simultaneous with George Skipper's design and construction of the Royal Arcade. While Mr Skipper was busy on Gentleman's Walk, it was his rival Edward Boardman who was working on the new Royal. Boardman was around twenty years older than Skipper, but

The Royal Hotel.

their careers overlapped and between them they've helped define much of the city's architecture. Something they had in common was a liking for the local stone known as Costessyware. Skipper used it for his own offices and the Jarrold building, and Boardman made a great flourish of it in the Royal Hotel's frontage.

For his builders Boardman chose John Youngs & Son, now part of the R. G. Carter Group. They'd worked on the railway station, which opened in 1886, just thirteen years before the Royal Hotel's grand opening on 17 November 1897.

In 1899, Jarrolds printed the official guidebook for the hotel, which listed the cost of rooms and facilities available. A visitor could take a suite from 15s, which included the room, a dressing room a sitting room and attendants.

The Hotel featured a 'Winter Garden' and the guide specifically mentions the main entrance as containing 'marbles of various colours' – a touch that may not have gone unnoticed by Skipper, who would famously use marble to such effect in the Norwich Union building he was commissioned to design a couple of years later in 1900.

When the twentieth century dawned the Royal Hotel rose with it. For decades it would be the first port of call for business leaders, politicians and the social elite. Stars working at Anglia TV across the road frequented the Royal. Campaigning cabinet and prime ministers stayed there. High-profile auctions and events were held in the hotel.

But, just as the Royal had been created to meet the demands of the railway age, sweeping away the old days of the coaching inns, it too would become the victim of changes in transport. For all its style and luxury the Royal lacked one important facility for late twentieth-century life: it didn't have a car park.

In an attempt to meet the changes in society the owners of the Royal proposed demolishing it and building a 'glass tower' in its place. It was a drawn out debate, but planning permission was refused. The glory days were over and a future as a hotel that couldn't cater for motorists was never a possibility. In an ironic twist, as the hotel's fortunes floundered, its neighbour and customers were flying. Anglia TV was expanding and needed more space. They took offices in the upper floors of the Royal Hotel building. By 1977 it wasn't a hotel any more, and it continues to be used as a commercial centre to this day.

Its purpose may have altered, but its edifice on Agricultural Hall Plain and its place in Norwich history is unchanged.

21. The Adam and Eve

The Adam and Eve deserves a place in in this book because of its age and historical significance. There's little doubt that, as old as it is, the current building contains nothing of the original inn. What stands today is largely seventeenth century in origin. As such, it's a charming and picturesque place that is much loved by tourists and residents. Close to the river, a short walk from the city's shopping and

Above and right: The Adam and Eve.

commercial centres and full of character, it's a joy. It's justifiably claimed to be the oldest pub in Norwich.

In terms of its place as a building in the history of Norwich, the Adam and Eve is very important indeed. Firstly, its origins stretch back to around 1249. Records suggest that this may have been a brewhouse operated by monks and delivering refreshment for the masons and builders working on the construction of Norwich Cathedral. Three hundred years later, in 1549, the Adam and Eve would be at the heart of the fighting during Kett's Rebellion. In Bishopgate a 1,500-strong royal army faced the rebels they had been sent to defeat. When a cavalry charge led by Lord Sheffield met with fierce resistance, his lordship was mortally wounded. He'd removed his helmet to signify his willingness to surrender, but being unrecognised by the rebels he was struck with a cleaver. They took him to the Adam and Eve, where he died.

22. The Britons Arms

Dating from 1420, this building stands in a part of Norwich defined by its antiquity. Perhaps one of the most picturesque streets in the country, Elm Hill runs from Princes Street down to Wensum Street, a few paces from the cathedral, the Maids Head and the Samson and Hercules. It's the most complete medieval street

Below and oppsite: The Britons Arms.

in Norwich. At its Princes Street end stands the fifteenth-century house that is home to the Britons Arms.

The building is a timeline for the city. With possible religious origins, its architecture has caused speculation. It seems to be resonant of Dutch methods, which, given the city's long connection with the Netherlands, is not unsurprising.

Timber-framed and thatched, it somehow survived the great fire of 1507, a blaze that destroyed most of the surrounding buildings and virtually all of Elm Hill.

Surgeons and wool merchants have occupied it. By the eighteenth century it was an inn or alehouse. It was as a pub that the name the Britons Arms first appeared.

After the Second World War the ancient building was acquired by the city council. It had been owned by Steward & Patterson, themselves a legendary part of Norwich brewing history. They sold it for a token £10.

The Britons Arms was a successful and popular coffee house and restaurant with a long track record by the early twenty-first century. In 2011, however, the city council put the building up for auction. The reality was that, as picturesque as it was, the building was in a bad and fragile state of repair. It was becoming unsafe. And it was becoming impossible to afford the repair costs.

Sue Skipper and Gilly Mixer were the leaseholders at the time. They'd run the place since the 1970s and their reaction to the possible sale was definitely not to give in. Up In Arms was the campaign they mounted; a campaign that defines Norwich and its spirit. Determined to see the building remain in public ownership, and operating as their café, they raised public awareness and support. It was a late decision, but it was a positive one. The council pulled back from auctioning the building. The Norwich Preservation Trust took it on a twenty-one-year lease and raised funds from English Heritage.

It's among the oldest buildings in the city, and even in the twenty-first century it echoes the radical and passionate spirit that has characterised its surroundings and people throughout history.

Education

23. The University of East Anglia

There had been discussions about creating a university in Norwich as far back as 1919, and it was back on the agenda in 1947. It would be April 1960, though, before the idea was given the go-ahead.

Just three years later – in the October of 1963 – the university was operational, albeit only for students of biological studies and English, and on a temporary site at the University Village. This was in reality a group of prefabricated buildings on the other side of the Earlham Road to where the university now stands.

In the meantime, in 1961 the university's first vice chancellor, Frank Thistlewaite, had asked Denys Lasdun to begin designs for a permanent

Above: The University of East Anglia's Grade II-listed Ziggurats.

Below: The university's Constable Terrace – built by R. G. Carter. (Courtesy of R. G. Carter Group Archive)

campus. Lasdun revealed his characteristic new brutalist designs by displaying a model at a press conference in 1963. It was another three years before the first buildings opened, and when they did there were noticeable differences to the original concept.

By 1968 Lasdun had been replaced as architect by Bernard Feilden. It was Feilden who added the 'square' or social space to Lasdun's designs, incorporating it into the scheme that included the teaching wall and residences that would become known as 'Ziggurats'.

Architecturally, the UEA has overcome early controversy and is now considered of real importance, with the Ziggurats now being Grade II listed. Academically, the university is world class. The Creative Writing course founded by Sir Malcolm Bradbury and Sir Angus Wilson in 1970 has established itself as the most respected of its kind in the UK. The Climatic Research Unit, which Hubert Lamb established in 1972, was a pioneer in climate change research. The National Student Survey, which ranks universities, features the UEA as the only such institution to be in its top five since the survey started.

The campus spreads across a swathe of land to the west of the city and encompasses the Sainsbury Centre for Visual Arts, Earlham Hall and the Enterprise Centre.

24. The Enterprise Centre

Located at the University of East Anglia, and a centre for student entrepreneurship, the Enterprise Centre firmly belongs in the 'Education' section of this book, and definitely deserves a place in a list of fifty buildings that define Norwich. It has less to do with the history of the city, but is very much part of the future.

The centre is one of the UK's most sustainable buildings. Constructed on a brown field site at the UEA, the Enterprise Centre was initially an academic exercise. It posed questions such as what would Britain's greenest commercial building look like? How could it be 'delivered'? And could it be used to kick-start or improve local trade and business?

The Adapt Low Carbon Group from the UEA approached the concept with the idea that there is 'another way to build'. In other words, they considered low carbon not just when the building would be in use, but the reduction of carbon impact during construction. In an echo of men like George Skipper, who had built in the city before, they used local materials. Combining natural and recycled materials with latest construction techniques, the building has proved to be a showcase in low-emission architecture.

The Enterprise Centre houses Enterprise Central, the university's student enterprise hub, supporting students and post-graduates aiming to start businesses.

Above and below: The Enterprise Centre. (Courtesy of David Kirkham, Fisheye Images)

From the outset the Enterprise Centre had a collaborative and innovative ethos. From day one the client and design team worked together, committed to achieving a demanding environmental specification. It proved to be a really important part of its success.

Outstanding architecture and design and a commitment to sustainable construction methods, materials and technologies have resulted in an exemplary building in which it is a joy to learn and work.

25. The Sainsbury Centre for Visual Arts

Norman Foster, later Lord Foster, was barely known as an architect when he was commissioned to design the Sainsbury Centre for Visual Arts. It's now seen as an important example of his early work.

He began the project in 1974 and it opened in 1978. A decade later, Foster would be called back to extend the building. He did it not by expanding it visibly, but by going downwards. His extension opened in 1991 and was contained in the slope of the site, featuring a curved glass front.

The purpose of the building was to create a home for the extraordinary collection of Robert and Lisa Sainsbury. Beginning with the purchase of Epstein's

The Sainsbury Centre for Visual Arts. (Courtesy of Oxyma)

bronze *Baby Asleep* in 1929, Sir Robert developed a passion for collecting that would evolve even further after he married Lisa van den Bergh in 1937. Avoiding transient fashions, refusing to have art given such labels as 'tribal' and often buying works from artists at the very start of their careers, the couple amassed what has become 'one of the few intact modernist collections of the 20th century'.

In 1973, Sir Robert and his wife gave the collection to the University of East Anglia, although they did not stop acquiring pieces. Lady Sainsbury would carry on collecting even after Sir Robert's death, and continued to do so until 2006.

It was the Sainsburys' son David who funded the building of a home for the collection, inevitably and appropriately, on the university's campus.

Norman Foster would acknowledge the support of the Sainsburys and the UEA as he developed his techniques of 'design development' and 'integrated design' for the construction of this massive, and massively impressive, building.

On the inside, the centre allows the display of 5,000 years of art in a stunning and accessible way. From the exterior it's a magnificent sight – so impressive that it's featured as the headquarters of Marvel's team of superheroes in the film *Avengers: Age of Ultron*.

Inextricably linked to the university and the city, the Sainsbury Centre for Visual Arts is justifiably a building of importance to the world – and, seemingly, beyond.

26. Norwich Technical Institute (Norwich University of the Arts)

With St Georges Street at its front and the River Wensum to its side, this big Victorian building is an important part of both the educational and artistic history of the city.

By the late nineteenth century the School of Art had been all too aware that its premises in the old Free Library were no longer fit for purpose. They were overcrowded and outdated, and students and staff alike were all too conscious of the need for change. The answer came in the form of the new Norwich Technical Institute Building.

Norwich's city engineer at the time was Mr Arthur Elliston Collins, and his name appears on the tablet commemorating the laying of the foundation stone in 1899. There is some evidence though that Mr Collins delegated the design work to his assistant, Mr W. Douglas Wiles. Exactly who did what is lost to history, but the building remains as an outstanding piece of late Victorian and into early Edwardian architecture. Its red brick and locally sourced terracotta seem to nod towards the style of George Skipper, who himself had studied at the Norwich School of Art, and features such as the heating certainly drew on the work of Mackintosh, who had designed the Glasgow School of Art.

The building employed the latest construction techniques, including steel and concrete in the floors and staircases.

There were problems along the way, however, and the Department of Science and Art put its foot down in 1898 demanding large single windows. The result was prolonged debate, arbitration and delay. But by 1901 the first classes were

Above and opposite: Norwich Technical Institute building.

Damien Hirst's 20-foot-high work *Hymn* is displayed here outside the building in St Georges Street in April 2018. Having been exhibited in some major cities around the world, the £2 million sculpture, weighing 6 tons, was displayed until July 2018 outside the Norwich University of the Arts.

held in the building. It seemed a 'barn of a place' to those who knew the old premises, but its simple and functional ideas about corridors linking studios and workrooms, its great tower and its innovative features all defined it as a statement, both architecturally and educationally.

Its place in education and the arts has continued. Today the building is one of ten in the area that make up the campus of Norwich University of the Arts.

27. All Saints Green Halls

In architectural contrast, the Norwich University of the Arts Student Accommodation Block at All Saints Green is a twenty-first-century addition to both the university and the Norwich landscape.

Designed exclusively for NUA and brought to fruition by Alumno Developments and Morgan Sindall, the building is a landmark development. Opened in 2015, it features over 200 en suite bedrooms in flats of between five to eleven rooms. A communal study area at the top of the building provides both a wonderful facility and stunning views across the city. The £10 million project involved not only the building of the nine-storey block, but also the refurbishment of the Grade II-listed No. 50 All Saints Green.

All Saints Green student accommodation. (Courtesy of Denisa Ilie)

As part of the city's important educational heritage, the building also stands as symbol of its constant development. Standing among the likes of Skipper's Marble Hall in Surrey Street, overlooking the bus station and close to the John Lewis building, it typifies the city's architectural diversity and the need to meet changing demands.

Museums

28. Strangers' Hall

Parts of this building can be traced back to the fourteenth century, and unsurprisingly it is Grade I listed. It's well known that is has been the home or 'residence' of mayors of Norwich, although the hall has also been occupied at various times by lawyers and a dance teacher.

The shape of Strangers' Hall has actually changed during its long life. It originally stood back from the street, but in the mid-fifteenth century it was rebuilt by William Barley, a local merchant. He positioned the upper storey so that it ran along the line of the street.

Various occupants added to and modified the building during the sixteenth and seventeenth centuries, although little has changed architecturally since then.

Two elements of the hall's history make the building important in the story of Norwich. Firstly, during the 1560s the city extended an invitation to around

300 Flemish people to come to Norwich. They were some thirty Flemish weavers with their families and friends, and the intention was to help revive the city's textile industry. More followed, driven by the religious persecution then rife in Europe. Within a few years the newcomers – or 'strangers' – represented around 30 per cent of the city's population. This was a demographic change made notable by its friendliness. Many of the original arrivals were given shelter by the then mayor, Thomas Sotherton, in his mayoral residence – hence the name Strangers' Hall.

The other aspect concerns the hall's later history and indeed the present. It's extraordinary to believe now, but by the mid-nineteenth century the hall was empty and effectively derelict. It had been acquired in 1797 by priests whose chapel had occupied the site where the Maddermarket Theatre now stands. When their tenure ended the house fell into disrepair, and at one point was on the verge of demolition. A property developer had bought it and saw potential in the site. Leonard Bolingbroke came to the rescue. A Norwich solicitor, Bolingbroke was treasurer of the Norwich Archeological Society and a very keen collector of antiques. He bought the hall and, after furnishing it from his own collection, opened it to the public in 1890 as the 'Folk Museum'.

In 1922, Bolingbroke presented the house and its contents to the city. By 1974 it had been officially included into the Norfolk Museums Service, and it is they who have steered it to its position today as one of the UK's most significant collections of artefacts representing domestic life.

Below and opposite: Strangers' Hall.

29. Museum of Norwich at the Bridewell

This building also began its life in the fourteenth century. It's known that it was the home of a merchant in 1325. Like Strangers' Hall, and indeed many of the buildings in this book, it is entwined in the history of the city and its development. Its origins are firmly in the prosperous trading times and textile boom of the mid-fourteenth century. It was modified and occupied by William Appleyard, who in 1403 became Norwich's first mayor.

Another mayor, Robert Gardener, owned the house in the sixteenth century, but at some point after his occupancy in 1580 it was sold to the city's Corporation. At that point the building took on a completely different role. Norwich was still in a period of commercial vibrancy and the population included many rich merchants. In contrast, and not unconnected, there was an 'underclass' of impoverished residents and itinerant beggars. In an attempt to avoid funding these people's existence by charity, the city established an initiative at the Bridewell.

Men were put to work on menial tasks such as cutting wood and women were set to spinning wool, but this was a harsh regime and whippings were commonplace. The Bridewell was, in effect, at best a house of correction, and in reality a prison.

It burned down in 1751. Legend has it that one prisoner, Peter Wildman, refused to seize the opportunity to escape and resolutely remained on the premises. It is Peter the Wildman who is still remembered in the name of a nearby pub.

Museum of Norwich at the Bridewell.

After rebuilding, it remained as a prison until 1828. During the rest of the nineteenth century and into the twentieth century the building was used for various purposes, all of them reflecting the developing story of Norwich. It served as snuff factory, a leather warehouse and eventually became part of the legendary Norwich shoe industry as Bowhill's shoe factory. And it was a connection with the shoe trade that would define the building's future. In 1923, Norwich shoe manufacturer Sir Henry Holmes bought the Bridewell and gave it to the city. He wanted it to be a museum and his aim was that it would 'provide a source of pleasure and pride to the citizens' and 'inspire the younger generation to realise the greatness of their heritage'. His ambition has been achieved, as today the Museum of Norwich at the Bridewell gives visitors a wonderful interactive insight into the working life of Norwich across the centuries

Religious Buildings

30. Norwich Cathedral

The construction of Norwich Cathedral began as early as 1096. The site chosen was on land that local Saxons used for their market, so resulted in the relocation of Norwich market to the site it occupies today. By 1145 the cathedral was essentially complete, although work continued for development and to make repairs after various damaging incidents. However, unlike the castle, there have been no major alterations to the building since the fifteenth century, when the stone spire was finally in place. Work was certainly needed to repair the damage caused by Puritan rioters in the Civil War. In fact, after the destruction of much of the contents in 1643 the cathedral was an empty ruin until the Restoration in 1660. Much later, in the 1830s, the south transept was renovated. The architect was Anthony Salvin who had been responsible for the sympathetic restoration work on Norwich Castle at around the same time.

That the cathedral and the castle – two great Norman buildings – are located within eyesight of each other is a clear indication of how important the city was, even as early as the eleventh century.

The building of the cathedral was actually initiated by Herbert de Losinga. The shape and allocation of dioceses had been evolving since the seventh century. By 1072 Thetford was a significant location, before its standing was transferred to Norwich. It was at this point that de Losinga bought the bishopric for £1,900 – a colossal sum at the time. He began his cathedral, which included a Benedictine monastery, two years later in 1096.

The cathedral precinct covered some 85 acres, which in the Middle Ages would have represented around 10 per cent of the city's entire area. The 'precinct' can be defined as the outmost boundaries of the monastery, and in today's geography stretches out across Tombland and the Close to the River Wensum.

Above and opposite: Norwich Cathedral.

It's difficult to overstate how impressive a building it is. Only Salisbury Cathedral has larger cloisters. The Norwich cloisters feature more than 1,000 bosses in the roof, hundreds of which are hand carved, painted and decorated. The Cathedral Close is one of the biggest and most populated in Europe.

There have been significant developments within the Close in the twenty-first century. The new award-winning refectory opened in 2004. In May 2010 the new hostry building was opened by HRH the Queen and the Duke of Edinburgh.

The lands and construction aside, Norwich Cathedral is inextricably linked with names from the city and the county's history. One of the gates – 'Ethelbert' – is named after an eighth-century saint and king of East Anglia. The other – Thomas Erpingham – was named after the benefactor who built it. He is buried at the cathedral. Lord Nelson went to school within the cathedral's grounds. When nurse Edith Cavell's body was eventually brought back to Norwich after her execution by a German firing squad in 1915, and after a ceremony at Westminster Abbey, it was at Norwich Cathedral that she was laid to rest.

Surviving plague, war and riots, Norwich Cathedral, like its close relative the castle, is one of the defining features of the Norwich skyline. Its continuing relevance and relationship with the city is marked by a small but important gift: the copper font used for baptisms has been worked from bowls used at the Norwich Rowntree Mackintosh factory, where they were used to make chocolate. It was given to the cathedral when the factory closed down in 1994.

31. Church of St Peter Mancroft

Of all the surviving medieval churches in Norwich, St Peter Mancroft is the largest. Perhaps one of the oddest things about the church is the fact that there is no saint known as Peter Mancroft. It is known that the church was dedicated to both St Peter and St Paul for a time, before it became named solely for Peter. As to 'Mancroft' little is known. Theories include a translation from the Latin for 'great field', and the possibility of it being named for a local landowner, but the real reason has slipped from recorded history.

The origins of the Church of St Peter Mancroft are in the eleventh century, coinciding with the period when the Normans moved the local market from the Tombland area to its current location to allow the construction of the cathedral.

The founder of the original church was the Earl of Norfolk, Ralph de Guader. Falling foul of William the Conqueror and losing his lands in a failed rebellion, de Guader effectively handed the church over to his chaplain – Wala – who, in those complicated times, delegated it further. On the run as a result of the rebellion's failure, Wala found himself in Gloucester and he bestowed the Church of St Peter to the abbey there. For the next three centuries the church known now as St Peter Mancroft was referred to as the Church of St Peter of Gloucester in Norwich.

By the late fourteenth century yet another body were in control of the church. Standing roughly where the Theatre Royal now exists was the Church of

Below and opposite: Church of St Peter Mancroft.

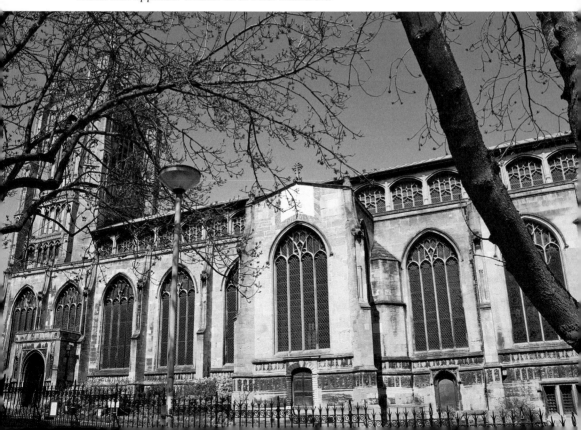

St Mary-in-the-Fields. It was this Benedictine dean and chapter who set about rebuilding St Peter's, and by 1430 a foundation stone was in place. This was now the era when Norwich enjoyed unprecedented status, demurring only to London.

The merchants and wealthy citizens of fifteenth-century Norwich built the Church of St Peter Mancroft as an unashamed reflection of the city's standing. It is a wonderful example of the Perpendicular style of architecture. The church is as noted for its light and airy interior, the result of there being no division between chancel and nave, as it is for its stonework, stained glass and wonderful hammer-beam roof.

The Victorian period saw further development and in 1896 the lead-covered spire was added to the tower. And it is the tower that houses St Peter Mancroft's other great claim to fame: its bells. St Peter Mancroft is of national and international significance in bell ringing. The first ever full peal of bells is attributed to the church – on 2 May 1715. It remains an important location for ringing, especially the art of 'change ringing'.

Steeped in history and a vibrant part of the present, St Peter Mancroft is an integral part of the story of Norwich.

32. St John the Baptist Cathedral

Westminster Cathedral is the only Roman Catholic cathedral in England that is larger than St John the Baptist in Norwich.

By the standards of cathedral building St John's is not ancient. It was begun in 1882 and completed in 1910. As is the case with so many of the city's great buildings, it occupies the site of a former establishment. It stands where the Norwich City Gaol once did.

One of the extraordinary things about this immense building is that it was, in effect, a gift to the city. Henry Fitzalan-Howard, 15th Duke of Norfolk, had succeeded to the dukedom when he was just twelve years old after the death of his father. He went on to have a notable public career, serving as postmaster general until 1900 when he gave up the role to serve in the Boer War. By then he'd also become mayor of Sheffield, where he would go on to be a freeman and lord mayor. He masterminded Sheffield's celebrations for Queen Victoria's Jubilee, became the first mayor of Westminster and served as a lieutenant colonel in the Second Boer War, during which he was wounded and sent home as a result.

For all his national and international service, it was to Norwich, his titular and ancestral city, that he turned when he decided to create something to mark his marriage to Lady Flora Hastings.

Fitzalan-Howard was a notable philanthropist and particularly known for his support of Roman Catholic projects, but this was enormous. The marriage was in 1877 and he announced that 'shortly after my most happy marriage, I wished to build a church as a thank-offering to God'. In 1882, he gave £200,000 – a phenomenal

St John the Baptist Cathedral.

figure at the time – to the Catholics of Norwich for them to begin the construction of St John the Baptist Church. (It would not become a cathedral until 1976.)

The chosen designer was George Gilbert Scott Jr, who also designed three of the colleges at the University of Cambridge. He was known for working in the late Gothic style, and St John's is testament to that. Its great tower, intricate stonework and magnificent glass mark it out as a supreme piece of late Victorian architecture. It's now a Grade I-listed building and central to the spiritual life of Norwich's Catholic community. Dominating the skyline at the top of the Unthank and Earlham roads, it's also a reminder of one man's enormous generosity.

33. St Julian's Church

Of all the churches in Norwich, this is one of the oldest. Due to suffering damage bordering on destruction in both the Reformation and the Second World War, it's difficult to be precise about when it was originally built, although some features indicate the eleventh century.

It's not the biggest church in Norwich by any means, but its place in the city's history is guaranteed by its connections to Julian of Norwich.

It is thought Julian was born in 1342. Julian was likely a woman from a prosperous family who after deciding to become an anchoress or hermit, lived in a

St Julian's Church.

cell adjoining this church. It is thought that it is from this church that she took the name Julian. In May 1373, while sufficiently ill to be receiving the last rites, she had visions that inspired her to write her *Revelations of Divine Love*.

Sealing herself away from the world, she lived the rest of her life here at St Julian's. There are doubts over the precise location of her cell, and there are gaps in our knowledge of her life. But, Julian of Norwich is acknowledged as one of the 'creative theologians, spiritual writers and mystics in the Christian tradition'. And, it's now generally agreed that the *Revelations of Divine Love* is the earliest surviving book written by a woman in the English language.

34. St Andrew's and Blackfriars' Halls

The family of Sir Thomas Erpingham, the 'hero of Agincourt' and benefactor of Norwich Cathedral, were generous contributors to the rebuilding of these halls. So, too, were another famous Norfolk family: the Pastons.

St Andrew's and Blackfriars' Halls stand within the city centre and somehow finding them always seems to be a surprise; their sheer size and antiquity create such a contrast with their immediate surroundings.

'The Halls', as St Andrew's and Blackfriars' Halls are now referred to, have been in the civic hands of Norwich since 1538. They are the most complete medieval

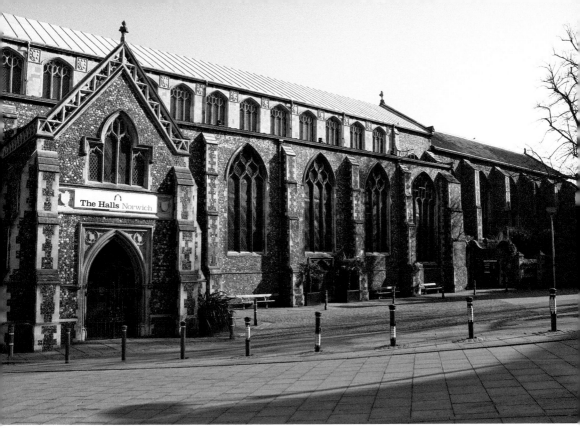

St Andrew's and Blackfriars' Halls.

friary complex still standing in England. Nowadays they host conferences and exhibitions, trade shows and private functions, but none of those were their original purpose.

The Friars of the Sack had come to Norwich from Marseilles and established a church and buildings on this site. In around 1307, the Dominican friars who had settled in the parish of Colegate seem to have taken over these buildings, which still in part exist as 'the Crypt'.

The Black Friars, as the Dominicans were called (because of the colour of their robes), were granted the properties by a royal licence under the condition that they looked after the last Friar of the Sack. They constructed new buildings only to see them destroyed by the great fire that destroyed much of the city in 1413.

The new church that they built was completed in 1470. Its nave was the building we know today as St Andrew's Hall. Blackfriars' Hall was part of the same complex. It was at this time of great rebuilding that the Paston family donated the gifts of beams for the roofs and the great doors that bear their arms. At the same time the family of Thomas Erpingham provided substantial funds. Erpingham's brother, Robert, was a friar within the church, which was doubtless part of their motivation. Their arms are also included in the architecture.

These great halls punctuate the history of Norwich over the next centuries. The city council bought them at the time of the Reformation to rescue them. They have served as granaries in the past, and were the first place of worship for local Nonconformists in the seventeenth century. By the late seventeenth century the halls were used to mint coins, and by 1712 the buildings had become the city workhouse. In 1859, a school was established in St Andrew's Hall. The Commercial School would be the precursor to the City of Norwich School, which would still be holding their 'Speech Days' there a century later.

Home to a part of the country's biggest civic portrait collection and now part of the 'Norwich 12' heritage series, these great halls have been part of the history of the city and today represent a vibrant element of its present.

Grand Houses

35. Earlham Hall

For an example of a house that is entwined with the history of Norwich, there are few better examples than Earlham Hall.

Located on the western edges of the city, it was built in 1642 by Robert Houghton. It would later be owned by Edward Bacon, who was a worthy but not spectacularly successful politician during the eighteenth century. As far as Earlham

Earlham Hall.

Hall is concerned, he is credited with creating a 'handsome, long, and lofty dining room'. When he died in 1786 the house passed to his nephew, Mr Bacon Frank, who lived in Yorkshire and rented it to the Gurney family.

During the Gurney family's long tenancy, which would last until the twentieth century, they made many changes to the architecture of the building. It is their contribution to history that makes them – and the house – so important.

To begin with, they were a successful family of wool merchants and part of the trade that generated so much of Norwich's wealth. They became wealthy themselves, to such an extent that in Gilbert and Sullivan's 1875 *Trial by Jury*, when one of the characters describes how he built up his fortune he claims that 'at length I became as rich as the Gurneys'.

Their riches did not impede their social responsibility. The Gurney wool business in Norwich's St Augustine's Street was sufficiently philanthropic to be known as 'the weavers' friend'. They extended their interests, rooted in the Quaker faith, to religion, politics and social reform.

Perhaps their most famous link to social reform is that of Elizabeth Fry. Born a Gurney and growing up at Earlham Hall, she married John Fry in 1800. Their wedding was at the Quaker Friends Meeting House in Goat Lane, Norwich. He was a Fry of the equally philanthropic and Quaker Fry's chocolate empire.

Elizabeth would go on to become one of the most ardent and successful campaigners for prison reform, which began with a prison visit to Newgate in 1813. Her achievements would be recognised in 2001 when she appeared on the Bank of England's £5 notes.

Mr Fry was a banker as well, as were the wealthy Gurneys. The Gurney Bank's merger with various London banks in 1896 would create the company we know today as Barclays.

The house appears in literature, most notably in *Lavengro* by George Borrow, who played and fished there as a boy in the early nineteenth century. John Gurney appears to have caught him there and took him into the house to show him his library.

In the twentieth century the biographer and art critic and Percy Lubbock spent summers there – his mother was the daughter of John Gurney. Lubbock's memoir *Earlham* won the James Tait Black Memorial Prize in the 1920s. And it was in the same century that the great house became part of the University of East Anglia, which stands adjacent to it. It had seen educational use before, serving as a temporary school while new premises were built in West Earlham. It had also, briefly, been a maternity home afer the one in Norwich had been bombed in 1942.

In 1963, the hall became the administrative offices and home of the vice chancellor of the new university. It would subsequently house the university's Law School and has undergone recent significant refurbishment.

Pop festivals and major concerts have been played out in Earlham Park and the hall has even been used as a backstage area for performers. It remains as inextricably linked to the history and life of Norwich as it always has.

36. The Assembly House

Within sight of the Church of St Peter Mancroft and probably on at least part of the land once occupied by the Benedictine community who rebuilt it, stands the Assembly House.

The building only became known as the Assembly House in 1950 after a £70,000 restoration project saw it reopen as a venue for 'the Arts and entertainment'. The works had been funded by H. J. Sexton, forging a link between the building and the Norwich shoe-manufacturing industry. However, connections to the city's trades can be traced much further back in this wonderful building's history.

In another direct association with the charter of 1404, which gave the city greater powers of self-governance, this was the site at which annual assemblies were held to elect the bailiffs who would administer and govern Norwich. At that point the building was used as a college for priests, having previously been a hospital that was founded in 1248 by John Le Brun as the Chapel and Hospice of St Mary-in-the-Field. This was also the location for another annual event: the Feast of Corpus Christi, a religious festival that was ultimately banned in 1548.

The ban of 1548 was part of Henry VIII's Dissolution and the chapel and hospice of St Mary-in-the-Field fell victim to it. After being taken over by the Crown the buildings were, in part, demolished. With the chapel, cloisters and choir gone, it was now a smaller and secular place. What was left of it was sold to the dean, but as a private dwelling.

After forty years or so in the ownership of Sir Thomas Cornwallis, the 'Chapel of the Field House', as he would call it, was bought by Sir Henry Hobart in 1609. By

The Assembly House.

1753 the site had changed hands again. Now leased to a group of aldermen, it was to become a place of 'entertainment for the county and the city'. To make the conversion they appointed Thomas Ivory as architect. It is his work that we see today.

Ivory would go on to make his mark on the city with other buildings. In 1754, assisted by the academic James Burrough, all his efforts were poured into a radical programme of demolition and rebuilding that would result in the House of Assemblies. 'Assemblies' of the great and good came to a stop in 1876 when the building became home to the Girls' Public School, which would become Norwich High School for Girls.

In 1939, the premises took on yet another role, serving as a camouflage school. It's safe to assume that it was during this period that Oliver Messel got to know the building. He was already established as a painter and theatrical set designer, and with the outbreak of war his talents were put to use as a camouflage artist. Among his achievements are the disguising of machine gun posts and pillboxes as haystacks, a castle and cafés. Presumably, he was assigned to the camouflage school to teach these techniques to others. He was certainly a leading campaigner after the war for the restoration of the House of Assemblies, and was instrumental in raising sufficient awareness for Sextons to provide their generous funding.

When the building reopened in 1950, as the Assembly House, it included the Noverre Cinema. Named after the family whose ballroom had once occupied the space, this small cinema is fondly remembered by generations of Norwich residents for its less than mainstream 'art house' screenings and altogether rather more sedate moviegoing experience.

The Assembly House would have another reopening some forty-five years later. A fire broke out in 1995. It took hold of the roof and ceilings and destroyed much of the restaurant, music room and entrance hall. Once again support for local business came to the rescue and two years later, in 1997, the place reopened in all the splendour we see today.

As a glimpse into the cultural history and significance of the Assembly House, it's interesting to note that it was here in 1805 that the city held the great ball to celebrate Nelson's legendary victory at Trafalgar. It was in these rooms too that the great dance innovations of the nineteenth century were first seen; the polka and the waltz were introduced here. And, as to famous visitors, we know for certain that Franz List played in these rooms.

37. Dragon Hall

Grade I listed and acclaimed as a gem of medieval architecture, Dragon Hall is also a site of archeological importance. Evidence suggests that there are traces of a Saxon dwelling beneath it.

Dragon Hall, as we know it, emerges around 1427 when a Robert Toppes built a trading hall on top of an earlier building. His addition was of timber with a crown post roof. It was decorated with carvings of fourteen dragons.

Above: Dragon Hall.

Left: The sign outside.

Toppes was, it seems, something of an entrepreneur and an ambitious merchant. His premises included access to the River Wensum (for his imports and exports), a warehouse, new stairways and what we can only assume was, in modern parlance, a lavish 'reception area'. By the time he was twenty-seven in around 1427 he was the city treasurer. Rising to become sheriff and mayor, he defines fifteenth-century Norwich commerce. He exported the local worsted cloth and imported everything from wine to spices.

Surviving some scandals, including a disputed election for the mayoralty, he had become one of the city's richest men by the mid-fifteenth century. Perhaps scared that his misdemeanours or his wealth would not stand him well in the final judgement, he made some very precise arrangements for his death. He'd already paid for a spectacular stained-glass window in the Church of St Peter Mancroft, but when he died in 1467 he also left bequests to all of the city's churches. And he included an instruction in his will that Dragon Hall should be sold, with the money to be used to pay priests to pray for his eternal soul.

The lofty, or mercenary, aim may have helped his soul, but Dragon Hall entered a less than happy period. After it was sold off it was converted into ever smaller dwellings. Toppes' impressive bay windows were lost and replaced by the doors and sash windows still in place today. It essentially became a tenement. Part of it was turned into the Old Barge pub, which for a while gave its name to the entire building. By the late 1890s it was home to 150 or more people, and in a very sorry state.

The tenements were eventually removed in Norwich's 1937 slum clearance programme, but, in a strange echo of Toppes' commerciality, by the 1950s the Old Barge pub was sharing the building with a butcher's shop and, perhaps reflecting his religiosity, there was also a rectory.

Eventually, after research and interest from historians, it became obvious that the building, despite its condition at the time, was of real historical and architectural interest. The Norfolk and Norwich Heritage Trust, created to manage the hall, worked with the city council, who had bought the building in 1979. They stripped away the walls and dividing panels that had so dramatically altered the interior. Floors and fireplaces were taken out, and over time the building regained something of its original appearance.

In 1986, it was officially renamed Dragon Hall and put into service as a community educational centre. The story would continue with further archeological work and research being carried out in the late 1990s and, thanks to a Heritage Lottery Fund grant, more improvements in 2006. The lift, offices and kitchen this provided allowed the hall to be used for business functions and weddings. Ten years later, in 2016, the Norfolk and Norwich Heritage Trust was wound up as the lease had been taken over by the Writers' Centre Norwich the previous year.

Dragon Hall is open to visitors and the Dragon Hall Heritage Volunteers are a fountain of knowledge, delivering tours and talks on its history. It's a building that has spanned the centuries, etching itself into the history of Norwich.

Commerce

38. The Agricultural Hall (Anglia House)

The post-war years had brought architectural change to Norwich, but another, cultural, phenomenon was about to appear: commercial television.

Anglia TV made its first broadcast on 27 October 1959, from the centre of Norwich. And it did it from within a building that, from the exterior, was totally incongruous with the new medium. The new studios were housed in the city's nineteenth-century Agricultural Hall.

First opening its doors in 1882, the Agricultural Hall had been built by J. W. Lacey of Norwich to host farmers' events and lectures. It provided a platform for speakers visiting Norwich, not least of who was Oscar Wilde. Surrounded by the cattle market, which would still be held in the city centre until well into the twentieth century, the hall was used as the trading floor for local agriculture. Livestock was brought in and corn and grain sales were negotiated there.

Decorations on the outside of this imposing Victorian building include the Prince of Wales feathers (referencing Prince of Wales Road, which runs from the hall to the railway station) and the city's crest, embellished to reflect the importance of agriculture to the city and county.

Anglia House, formerly the Agricultural Hall.

Over its long life the hall has been used as a roller-skating rink and as a wartime sorting office for Royal Mail – the main post office was next door in Hardwick House. The legendary tightrope walker Blondin also appeared there. None of these uses could have been foreseen by local MPs (including J. J. Colman, who commissioned the building), nor by J. B. Pierce, the architect. His terracotta edifice was a statement of agricultural importance for nineteenth-century Norwich. And yet, not long after its opening, the Agricultural Hall would be the location for a thrilling new form of entertainment that would prove to be an ironic link with its eventual occupants.

In January 1887 the hall was hosting George Gilbert's Circus of Varieties. As part of the programme the audience were presented with 'Animated photographs representing with marvellous accuracy scenes from everyday life'. They were films. An amazed Norwich audience witnessed what was, in effect, the city's first cinema screening.

Watching that night and seeing moving pictures of trains, the Derby, a boxing kangaroo and the Prince of Wales at a garden party, the citizens of Norwich were amazed. In what must be some of the earliest filmed sports coverage, they saw local hero Jem Mace in a boxing bout. Nearly 150 years later the same building would see the launch of, and become home to, a new TV company – the medium that would, for a while at least, effectively ruin the cinema industry whose birth they were witnessing.

Eventually, the Agricultral Hall would be renamed Anglia House, when it became the headquarters of Anglia TV. The company would construct a modern – for 1959 – TV studio inside the outer fabric of the Victorian hall. It's an imposing building with an important place in the commercial and cultural history of Norwich.

39. Hardwick House

The Post Office stamped their name on the building, but the crowns on it were from the original occupants: the bank.

The official address of Anglia House is still Agricultural Hall Plain. It's a location it shares with the neighbouring Hardwick House, named after its designer, Philip Hardwick. Hardwick was the son, and grandson, of successful architects. At the time of being commissioned to design this Norwich building he was acting as architect to the Bank of England. It must have made him an obvious choice as the building that was to take his name was to be the head offices of the Crown Bank.

Harvey & Hudson's Crown Bank opened in 1792. By the 1860s, Sir Robert Harvey, 1st Baronet of Crown Point and grandson of the founder, was running the business. He had been elected as the Conservative MP for Thetford in the 1865 general election and appeared to be the perfect example of a late nineteenth-century businessman and a pillar of society. He had rebuilt his house at Crown Point, the seat of his baronetcy, and, with the bank operating successfully out of branches throughout Norfolk and Suffolk, he commissioned Hardwick House.

Above: Hardwick House.

Below: Detail on the building.

It was opened in 1866, and it was elaborate. The neoclassical styling, impressive entrance and dominant position at the top of Prince of Wales Road were everything expected of a flourishing bank, headed by a successful local businessman and politician.

The problem was that Sir Robert was not as astute as he appeared. He was speculating on the Stock Exchange, and he was losing money. Greatly concerned about his reputation, he concealed his losses by recording them as debts of fictitious customers of the bank. It was, however, a fraud that was not destined to last. By 1870 the market was falling further – largely as a result of the outbreak of the Franco-Prussian War. With his debts running into hundreds of thousands of pounds, Harvey could no longer conceal the truth. On 19 July 1870, just four years after the opening of Hardwick House, Sir Robert Harvey went to his house at Crown Point and shot himself.

The bank could not survive the scandal, and it failed. Panic broke out. In an attempt to stabilise the situation and bring some calm to the city, Gurneys Bank bought the goodwill of the Crown Bank.

The Post Office moved into Hardwick House and would remain there for decades. To meet the demands of wartime mail they would share space in the Agricultural Hall, their newer next-door neighbour.

It's one of those oddities of history that, across generations, many people have assumed that the crown motifs in the architecture of Hardwick House represent the General Post Office, or Royal Mail – an emblem of one of society's most dependable services. In reality, however, they were a reference to the name of the bank that commissioned the building, suffered from fraud, and collapsed there.

40. Surrey House, the 'Marble Hall' of Aviva

Aviva was known by its original name of Norwich Union from its formation in 1797 until 2008. Thomas Bignold, a local banker and merchant, was still in his thirties when he founded the Norwich Union Society for the Insurance of Houses, Stocks and Merchandise from Fire. In 1808 he would launch the Norwich Union Life Insurance Society.

The business would grow and prosper until, by the dawn of the twentieth century, it was a worldwide operation. It was in the early years of that century – between 1900 and 1904 – that Norwich Union commissioned and built the spectacular Surrey House.

Their choice of architect was the redoubtable George Skipper. Having already made his mark on Norwich with the Royal Arcade, which had opened the previous year, Skipper would now make some choices that would create a statement building and define the company.

His first exciting decision was to use a spectacular consignment of marble. He had discovered that a significant quantity of Italian marble had been imported for use in Westminster Cathedral. For various reasons it was not to be deployed and

Surrey House.

Above and right: Inside Surrey House – the 'Marble Hall' of Aviva.

Dwarfed now by its modern neighbours, the building is still central to Norwich's Aviva complex.

Skipper, aware that it could now be bought at a favourable price, persuaded the board of Norwich Union to buy it for him to use. From this he created the forty massive columns of the main hall.

Drawing on influences as diverse as the Temple of Solomon and Masonic symbolism, Skipper brought in Italian artisans and then modern specialists to create a building that at one and the same time had the gravitas of antiquity as well as the latest facilities. These included a prototypical air-conditioning system, driven by a pendulum. Made to look like a marble fountain, the device pulled in air from the outside, controlling its temperature by fans and radiators. The effect was to keep the building warm in winter and cool in summer (despite the marble interior).

Conceived as a working headquarters, Surrey House had all the necessary offices, meeting rooms and board rooms. It was also laden with themes that underpinned the need for prudency and insurance. Paintings were strategically placed to show the security of families who protected themselves and the dangers that would befall those who didn't.

Although effectively completed in 1904, work would carry on until 1912, fashioning the dazzling interior to the externally imposing offices.

Standing on Surrey Street, the building is central to the Aviva operations to this day, and has become surrounded by the company's later offices. As imposing as the modern buildings are they have not diminished the bold, stunning statement that George Skipper had made for Norwich Union.

41. George Skipper's Offices

Skipper was very good at making statements. By 1904, when the main work on Surrey House was being completed, he has also finished a project conceived to say something about him, rather than his clients.

His practice had grown greatly, with some fifty staff now on the payroll. His order book was full and Norwich alone had extremely visible evidence of his skill and style. At almost forty, with the world at his feet, he decided to establish new office premises for his business. The result was No. 7 London Street.

Once again his choice of materials was a vital element in the plan. Guntons of Costessey were his chosen suppliers for their magnificent terracotta, which was very fashionable and ideal for the contemporary style he wanted. This was more than an office building; it was an advertisement for his business.

George Skipper's offices.

Skipper's reliefs were a clear indication of his business as an architect.

The rules at the time prohibited architects from promoting their business with signage on their buildings. George Skipper found an interesting way around that: set into the terracotta façade of No. 7 London Street are some exquisite reliefs depicting trades associated with the design and construction of buildings. At first sight they are decorative panels, wholly appropriate to the art nouveau building. Upon reflection, however, they're also a clear indication that this is the office of an architect.

Just as he had for Norwich Union in Surrey House, George Skipper made sure that his office had every imaginable facility for modern commerce and it incorporated the very latest in heating and lighting.

Its façade has remained impressive, still retaining the deep-red colour of the terracotta. Inside the building today there is a 'Skipper Room', dedicated to the man who traded from there and curated by the current occupants – Jarrolds.

42. Westlegate Tower

The Bonds, or John Lewis, building had been a symbol of 1950s modernity and its near neighbour would deliver the same cultural shift for the 1960s. Originally built as Westlegate House and begun in 1959, when it opened in 1961 it was instantly one of Norwich's tallest buildings and absolutely striking in its style.

Westlegate Tower.

With eleven floors and reaching 33 metres in height, it was the work of Chaplin & Burgoine. Architect Robin Burgoine, working with Norwich construction company Lushers, built the tower and pushed back boundaries. His design was more modern, more adventurous, than the original idea for the site, and in truth caused some controversy. While Pevsner and Wilson in their *The Buildings of England* referred to is as 'the city's first tower block' and 'a better attempt to fit a modernist building into a tight townscape setting than was apparent in work immediately after the war', one local journalist called the building 'Burgoine's glass tower', a phrase redolent of contemporary, conservative, criticism.

By the mid-1960s it was inevitable that the city's teenagers would frequent the café on the ground floor. This was modern city life and it suited the generation perfectly. And yet, somehow, the building, for all its modernity, seemed to fade for a while. Branded by some as an eyesore, it was as if the problem was not the building but the neglect of it.

Photographs of the tower during its construction would take on an eerie resonance in 2014. A refurbishment programme by F. W. Properties meant that it was once again covered in scaffolding. Suddenly it looked like it had in 1959. When it re-emerged, complete with a new penthouse, which increased its height to 41 metres, it was a desirable address. Perhaps Mr Burgoine had been ahead of his time.

43. Prospect House

Well within the sweep of the city centre, but in stark contrast to the Victorian buildings, not to mention Norman castle, stands Prospect House. Home to local newspapers, including the *Eastern Evening News* and *Eastern Daily Press*, the building is in fact the headquarters of Archant. The company is now the largest multimedia business of its kind in the UK, producing regional newspapers, magazines and digital material.

Although Prospect House is a 1960s building, the company has its roots in the nineteenth century – the era of Victorian entrepreneurs and innovation that produced so much of the city's buildings and commerce.

Thomas Jarrold and Jeremiah Colman, along with Jacob Tillett and John Coleman, launched the *Norfolk News* in 1845. The *Eastern Daily Press* and *Eastern Evening News* would emerge from the company. The business moved premises more than once, until settling for many years into offices at Redwell Street.

By the late 1960s it was apparent that bigger and ideally custom-built offices were necessary. Yates, Cook & Derbyshire were the architects of Prospect House. Commissioned in 1968 and demonstrably modern in design, the new building featured flint in its facings as a direct reference to local heritage.

Seen as brutalist by some, the building opened in 1970, heralding an era of growth and diversification for the company that would become Archant in 2002.

If the building itself created an impact when it opened in 1970, so too did the sculpture that stands by its entrance. Bernard Meadows was one of Britain's most important twentieth-century sculptors. Born in Norwich, he'd studied at the Norwich School of Art before becoming Henry Moore's first assistant in 1931. Although he returned to working with Moore after his war service, Meadows developed his own career and exhibited widely, producing a vast amount of art for both private collections and public commission.

The *Eastern Daily Press* commission he named, simply, *Public Sculpture* is said to be his greatest work. It is definitely his largest work.

Public Sculpture features huge blocks of stone, combined with metal balls. The 'dimples' in the metal are perhaps the reason for some of the work's controversy, with some people seeing anatomical references in them.

Meadows died when he was ninety in 2005. At the time of writing there is talk of Archant moving premises again. Whatever happens at Prospect House the city will still have an imposing twentieth-century building, with a significant piece of public art at its doors.

Prospect House.

44. No. 24 Cattle Market Street – The Crystal House

This building deserves a place in this collection, even though historic details on it are scant. Even its date of construction is something of a mystery. Some listings show it as having been built in 1868, although the structure itself carries the date '1863'. What is certain is that the design was influenced by London's Crystal Palace, which was built to house the Great Exhibition of 1851. The Norwich building became known as the Crystal House and was built for Holmes & Sons, a firm of machine engineers.

It served for some years as the home of Panks, another Norwich engineering and electrical company, whose name once featured in prominent letters across the frontage. Two storeys tall with full-height windows adorned with iron-glazed columns, it's a triumph of the Victorian industrial age. Early illustrations show the building as larger than now, stretching further back, but it has been suggested that this might have been due to artistic licence or an original design rather than its actual size.

The Crystal House was damaged by wartime bombing and suffered further indignity years later when trees fell on it. On both occasions it was sympathetically repaired.

By the 1990s it was in use as a toy and model shop and it would subsequently become a furniture store. When, in 2016, the city council refused permission to

No. 24 Cattle Market Street – The Crystal House.

demolish the building at its rear it claimed that such a plan would 'result in the loss of historic fabric' of the building. Much debate about the building's future and possible development saw the furniture company Warings move out.

Comments made during the discussions on the building included the statement that plans should 'preserve and enhance the architectural and historic character of the important early survival of an iron and glass showroom'. Which is why No. 24 Cattle Market Street, or the Crystal House, is in this collection of fifty buildings – because of its architecture and its commercial heritage.

45. St James Mill

This mill took three years to build and the man behind it had a single intention. Samuel Bignold was the youngest son of Thomas Bignold, who had founded the Norwich Union Fire Insurance Society in 1797, which grew into what we now know as Aviva. Samuel worked for his father's company and was secretary to the Norwich Union Fire Insurance Society, as well as its sister company the Norwich Union Life Assurance Society. He held public office and served as Sheriff of Norwich in 1830, and as mayor more than once between 1833 and 1872.

In 1833, he'd established the Norwich Yarn Company. As mayor of Norwich he saw the establishment of a company 'for the spinning of yarn, on a scale calculated to give extensive employment to the poor', as a means of reducing unemployment at the same time as reviving the Norwich textile industry. The Norwich textile

Right and below: St James Mill.

industry, once the backbone of the city's commerce, was then flagging. Better production methods in other parts of the country had created serious competition. The changes in trade rules after 1815 had further impacted on the traditional methods used in the city.

Bignold's idea was broadly welcomed and no time was lost in implementing it. Schemes were put in place to raise the money and by September 1834 a site had been chosen and purchased. The land, by the river at Fishergate, is on the site known as Whitefriars, which is named after the Carmelite Friars who had settled there before the Norman Conquest.

The plans were ambitious. A sum of £20,000 was to be raised and, after the land was purchased, some £3,500 was to be allocated for buying machinery. Hundreds would be employed in a mill with thirty spinning frames. The great mill would supply vast quantities of yarn to the city's weavers. The textile trade would be saved and unemployment would fall. The Poor Rate would therefore be called on less.

And so it was amid great celebrations that the foundation stone was laid in 1836, and the city watched as the building took shape. The great chimney grew ever skywards, but profits didn't. Despite all of the activity and the opening of the completed building in 1840, trade was not good. Companies were collapsing, throwing large quantities of cheap yarn onto the market. Slowly the truth emerged. From the outset, Bignold and his fellow directors had been secretly borrowing to keep the business afloat. It couldn't carry on forever. By 1850 it was all over. The Norwich Yarn Company collapsed under the weight of almost £40,000 worth of debt.

The building, though, despite a fire in 1846, remained intact. It would become a mill again under various owners, including Joseph Park who let out floors to tenants. Park died in 1893 but his heirs had no long-term ambitions for it.

In 1901 Jarrolds were seeking premises because their printing works was expanding. William and Herbert Jarrold paid a £200 deposit against an £8,000 price for the mill, acquiring more space than they really wanted and much equipment that they didn't need.

The Joseph Park company remained though, paying rent for four floors. When they left in 1905 another legendary Norwich name – Caleys – moved in. Before then, Jarrolds had already converted much of the premises for printing, giving them the opportunity to move their print operation out of the London Street premises, leaving the way clear for George Skipper to work his magic and create the department store as we know it.

Caleys carried on in St James Mill as tenants of Jarrolds, making crackers and boxes for their chocolates until 1920. When they left, Jarrolds were approached by the Ministry of Works. There was an eerie resonance with Bignold's original pan for the mill in the proposed scheme. The idea was to rent space in the mill to create a 'Government Instructional Factory'. It was about providing employment.

This time, though, the objective was to help train men who had become disabled in the First World War and were therefore unemployable. The sticking point was that Jarrolds were not happy about the rental agreement and eventually sold the mill to the government for £25,328 – a handsome return on the £8,000 expenditure of less than twenty years earlier.

Although successful – it trained thousands of men across the country in similar factories – the scheme did not last forever. The government would continue to use St James Mill until 1933, but as the scheme wound down they sold the premises in 1927. They sold it back to Jarrolds.

Jarrolds continued to grow their printing business at the mill and produced work for the government during the Second World War. After the war the company grew further, installing innovative equipment such as the then largest full colour litho plant in 1948. Magazine printing in the 1970s saw more expansion.

It was Jarrolds who refurbished St James Mill in 1991, creating office accommodation that could be let out. Although the company ceased as a printer in 2005 the mill now houses the John Jarrold Printing Museum, and is home to Jarrold Training.

St James Mill is a twenty-first-century commercial hub, focused on today and the future. It stands as an impressive reminder of so much of the city's commercial and industrial heritage.

Shops

46. The Royal Arcade

Very much in the heart of the city, this construction is not entirely visible at first sight. The Royal Arcade runs from Gentleman's Walk to Castle Street and stands on the site once occupied by The Angel coaching inn.

What we know today as Gentleman's Walk was the location of several inns, each with its own lengthy yard stretching to the street still named 'Back of the Inns'. These were lively, sociable places. They thrived as the city thrived as a fashionable Georgian centre and provided accommodation, entertainment, stabling and, certainly in the case of The Angel, a venue for public meetings and headquarters of the Whig party.

The Angel survived until 1840 when it was sold and, like so many places at the time, renamed The Royal to mark the marriage of Victoria and Albert.

The Royal was part of a new era. The Victorian railway boom was in full swing and the old coaching routes were disappearing, along with the inns that served them. With London now more accessible, the hotels needed to offer a more comfortable, sedate experience. And they needed to make an impression.

The Gentleman's Walk entrance to the Royal Arcade is evidence of that. This is the rebuilt 1846 frontage to The Royal, which was left intact when the hotel moved to the top of Prince of Wales Road in 1897 to be nearer the railway station.

The following year, Norwich-based architect George Skipper, at the time in partnership with his brother, took on the commission to build the Royal Arcade.

The Royal Arcade.

Above left: The angel atop the arcade is a reference to the old Angel Inn.

Above right: The Royal Arcade.

Neither he nor the builders lost any time. The Royal Arcade was officially opened on 25 May 1899. Arts and Crafts in style, it met with instant approval. The local press started by saying: 'The general view of it is pleasing in the extreme, and there can be no doubt it will prove a permanent attraction to visitors, no less than to the townsfolk.' When they got into their stride the newspapers went further. It was, they said, as if something from 'the Arabian Nights had been dropped into the heart of the city'.

It was an understandable reaction. Inside the entrance created from the old hotel front the new arcade was a vision. Two storeys high and 75 metres long, it was Norwich's answer to London's Burlington Arcade. Shopfronts ran its length and a glazed roof let light flood in. Gorgeous green tiles had been made by Doulton and were decorated by W. J. Neatby, who had worked on Harrods food hall. This was luxury shopping and in the most stylish of settings. Skipper, whose work features so prominently in Norwich, had worked his magic once more.

In this most modern of late nineteenth-century designs, Skipper had left a subtle and touching reference to the city's past. At the Castle Street end of the arcade he designed his own entrance to complement the existing one on Gentleman's Walk. Into the dramatic construction he incorporated a figure. A figure of an angel.

47. Jarrolds

The Jarrolds store building dominates the corner of London Street and is a vital part of Norwich's commercial history. Skipper's offices are now part of the premises occupied by the department store. They had been on the site since 1840, but the building as we know it today is largely the 1903 work of their 'next door neighbour' George Skipper.

His work was a triumph again. Creating a stately look while leaving no doubt that this was a store, he adapted classical styles, including the Ionic for the upper levels. This was clever as the style was linked to wisdom and Skipper was using it to reflect Jarrolds connections to books.

In a twist that was plainly related to his work on his own offices next door, he incorporated into this Ionic statement some reliefs, or cartouches, of people's names. On his own building he'd reflected the trades of building; for Jarrolds he featured the names of authors they'd published.

Skipper would carry out substantial remodelling of the London Street and Exchange Street corner frontage in 1923.

The records show that the relationship between the city's leading architect and its primary retailer was a strained one. Exterior flourishes designed by Skipper were not entirely accepted by Jarrolds. His presence in the store caused tension. However, the building stands as another part of the Skipper legacy, an integral

Jarrolds.

Skipper used reliefs again for the Jarrolds store, this time referencing the authors that Jarrolds had published.

part of Norwich city centre and the home of one of the country's most important independent department stores.

With the growth and development of the store Jarrolds have taken over more of the buildings bordered by London Street, Exchange Street and Little London Street, absorbing and preserving George Skipper's offices as they've done so. They have also created a successful modern business on almost exactly the site of the shop opened by their founder when he came to Norwich, from Woodbridge, in 1823. Little London Street was then known as Cockey Lane and it was here that John Jarrold and his son opened their doors. They had arrived, well prepared, with substantial funds in cash. They deposited it in Gurneys Bank.

48. Debenhams

The shop known today as Debenhams will for some local people always be remembered as Curls. The Curl brothers were briefly in partnership with another Norwich retailing family, the Buntings, but they soon went their own way and by 1900 had established a sizeable department store where the current building stands on Orford Place and Brigg Street.

The original building was destroyed by bombing in the air raids of 1942. The resulting crater would be a scar on Norwich city centre for the next decade.

Debenhams.

Used variously as a water tank and car park, it became the subject of an often repeated question: 'when will they fill in the hole?'

Local firm T. Gill & Son had completed the building work by 1956 and the much vaunted new store opened that spring. Its 97,000 square feet of floor space bristled with modern features, including an escalator, a lift and air conditioning.

The Debenham Group took over Curls during the 1960s, but it wasn't until 1973 that the name changed. Today this 1950s building, with a decidedly pre-war 1930s style, still dominates the site of the original store. A landmark building in its own right, it's also a symbol of how the city rose from the darkest days of the Second World War to forge new generations of commerce.

49. John Lewis

If Norwich folk of a certain age think of Debenhams as Curls, then they also think of John Lewis as Bonds. Like Curls, the Bonds store had been destroyed during the Second World War bombing, along with the cinema next to it. In a twist of history, the new building was designed by Robert Owen Bond, who was working in his father's architectural practice and was a direct descendant of Robert Herne Bond, who had founded the Bonds shop as a drapers in 1879.

John Lewis.

The stylish and sweeping frontage of the new store was absolutely right for the post-war world. Completed in 1951, it represented modern retailing and architecture at the same time. Dominating All Saints Green and soon to be joined in the city's new styling by Westlegate Tower, the building is as impressive in the twenty-first century as it was at its opening.

The Bonds name would eventually disappear in 2001, despite having been acquired by John Lewis nearly twenty years earlier.

To Conclude

50. The Jarrold Bridge

As the last building to be featured – because a bridge can be considered a building – and in a section of its own, is the Jarrold Bridge.

Seemingly floating above the water on its two delicate columns, the Jarrold Bridge is some 80 metres long. It crosses the River Wensum at a point just beyond the Adam and Eve, connecting with the St James Place development on the other bank.

Architects Ramboll conceived a bridge that was 'slender, with sweeping curves derived from the unique features of the site' and steelwork contractors S. H. Structures fabricated the design in five sections, allowing easier transport to the site.

Jarrold Bridge.

The bridge was the idea of Peter Jarrold when he was chairman of Jarrold & Sons, whose printing works occupied the site. In fact, the site's redevelopment allowed Mr Jarrold's concept to become a reality. The bridge bears his name.

Crossing the river between the city's oldest inn and some of its newest business premises, the Jarrold Bridge somehow typifies the ever-changing, ever-progressing nature of Norwich. It literally joins the old and new quarters of the city, forming a link that characterises this city as somewhere determined to reach for the future without losing sight of its past. It's a connection; a link in the story of Norwich. Which is why it's a fitting conclusion to this collection, this story of Norwich in fifty buildings.

Acknowledgements

As ever, in writing this book I have needed and received help from several quarters. Thanks are due to my lifelong friend, the architect Andrew Armes, who discussed the project with me at the outset and in particular guided me towards the Enterprise Centre, which we, with Jo and Sue, very much enjoyed visiting. The Enterprise Centre staff were extremely helpful and special thanks are due there to Penny Wright for her help and David Kirkham for the photographs.

Thanks are also due to Caroline Bailey and the team at Norwich University of the Arts; R. G. Carter Archives for all their help; to Anna Stone, group archivist at Aviva, for her permission to take photographs; and I really want to give a mention to my friend and fellow writer Edward Couzens-Lake for his help.

I've credited photographs where appropriate and I'm confident that I've not used any pictures without permission. If you see an image here that you consider your property I can only say that I did my utmost to track you down and acknowledge ownership, and if I didn't find you I've used your work in good faith and without malice.

Thanks go to Martin Figura for the picture of me.

All pictures are otherwise by me. At which point I have to give a special mention and thanks to my daughter Katie and son-in-law Ben for the loan of their camera – thanks Katie and Ben.

My thanks go to the team at Amberley Publishing for their constant help and support. And to everybody else who in any way helped me write this book, I say a heartfelt 'thank you'.

As ever, I have to give special thanks to my wife, Sue. Without her constant support none of this would ever happen.

About the Author

Pete Goodrum is a Norwich man. He has had a successful career in advertising, working on national and international campaigns, and now works as a freelance advertising writer and consultant.

Pete is also a successful author. Among his books, published by Amberley, *Norwich in the 1950s*, *Norwich in the 1960s* and *Norfolk Broads: The Biography* have all topped the local bestseller charts.

He makes frequent appearances on BBC local radio, covering topics ranging from advertising to music, and from local history to social trends. He's also a TV presenter, having written and presented documentaries.

A regular reader at live poetry sessions and actively involved in the media, Pete has a real passion for the history of Norfolk and Norwich. And he's a prolific public speaker. He lives in the centre of the city with his wife, Sue.

The author, Pete Goodrum, on Mousehold Heath, Norwich. (Photo by Martin Figura)